CREATING BUSINESS MODELS:

A GUIDE FOR ENTREPRENEURS, DISRUPTORS, AND PIONEERS

BY

TONY I. SCHMIDT

Copy © right 2024

CREATING BUSINESS MODELS:

A GUIDE FOR ENTREPRENEURS, DISRUPTORS, AND PIONEERS

In today's dynamic market, crafting a robust model is essential for entrepreneurs, disruptors and pioneers. This guide provide a concise roadmap to designing models that capture values through innovative products and service

TONY I. SCHMIDT

Table of Contents

Cover page 3
Title page 3
CHAPTER 1. 5
INFORMATION ON BUSINESS MODELS 5
   UNDERSTANDING THE BASICS OF BUSINESS MODELS 5
      THE IMPORTANCE OF BUSINESS MODELS IN
      ENTREPRENEURSHIP 9
CHAPTER 2. 14
THE FOUNDATIONS OF BUSINESS MODEL DEVELOPMENT 14
   IDENTIFYING MARKETING OPPORTUNITIES 14
      DEFINING VALUE PROPOSITIONS 17
CHAPTER 3. 26
TYPE OF BUSINESS MODELS 26
CHAPTER 4. 43
DESIGNING YOUR BUSINESS MODEL CANVAS 43
CHAPTER 5. 56
REVENUE STREAMS AND PRICING STRATEGIES 56
   MONETIZATION MODELS: EXPLORING REVENUE STRATEGIES
   56
CHAPTER 6. 66
BUILDING SUSTAINABLE COMPETITIVE ADVANTAGE 66
   DIFFERENTIATION STRATEGIES: CREATING VALUE AND
   COMPETITIVE ADVANTAGE 66
      CREATING BARRIERS TO ENTRY: SECURING COMPETITIVE
      ADVANTAGE 71

CHAPTER 7. 77
SCALING AND GROWTH STRATEGIES........77
CHAPTER 8. 88
BUSINESS MODEL INNOVATION AND ADAPTATION........88
RESPONDING TO MARKET CHANGES: STRATEGIES FOR BUSINESS AGILITY........89
PIVOTING STRATEGIES: NAVIGATING CHANGE WITH AGILITY........94
CHAPTER 9. 101
CASE STUDIES AND REAL-LIFE EXAMPLES........101
SUCCESSFUL BUSINESS MODEL INNOVATIONS: DRIVING GROWTH AND COMPETITIVE ADVANTAGE........102
CHAPTER 10. 113
FUTURE TRENDS IN BUSINESS MODEL DEVELOPMENT........113
CHAPTER 11. 127
CONCLUSION AND FINAL THOUGHTS: EMBRACING CHANGE AND DRIVING INNOVATION........127

CHAPTER 1.

INFORMATION ON BUSINESS MODELS

Business models outline how a business creates, delivers, and captures value. They encompass the strategy and structure necessary for sustainable revenue generation. Effective business models align products or services with customer needs while ensuring profitability and competitive advantage.

UNDERSTANDING THE BASICS OF BUSINESS MODELS

A business model serves as the foundation upon which an organization operates, defining how it creates, delivers, and captures value. At its core, understanding the basics of business models entails grasping the fundamental concepts that drive revenue generation, market positioning, and sustainability.

Value Proposition:

Central to any business model is the value proposition, which articulates the unique benefit or solution offered to customers. This could be a product, service, or combination thereof that addresses a specific need or pain point in the market. A clear and compelling value proposition is essential for attracting and retaining customers.

Customer Segments:

Identifying the target audience or customer segments is crucial for tailoring products or services to meet their specific needs. Understanding the demographics, preferences, and behaviors of these segments enables businesses to refine their offerings and marketing strategies effectively.

Revenue Streams:

Revenue streams represent the avenues through which a business earns income from its value proposition. This could include one-time sales, recurring subscriptions, licensing fees, or advertising revenue. Diversifying revenue streams can enhance stability and long-term growth prospects.

Cost Structure:

Every business incurs costs in delivering its value proposition and operating its activities. Understanding the cost structure involves identifying fixed and variable expenses, such as production costs, marketing expenses, overheads, and personnel salaries. Optimizing costs is critical for maintaining profitability and competitiveness.

Channels:

Channels refer to the various methods by which a business reaches and interacts with its customers. These could include online platforms, retail stores, direct sales teams, or partnerships with distributors. Effective channel management ensures seamless customer experiences and maximizes market reach.

Key Activities and Resources:

Key activities encompass the core functions and processes that drive the delivery of the value proposition. This could involve product development, manufacturing, marketing campaigns, customer support, and logistics. Adequate resources, including financial, human, and technological assets, are essential for executing these activities efficiently.

Partnerships and Key Relationships:

Collaborations with suppliers, distributors, technology providers, and other stakeholders can significantly impact a business's success. Building strong partnerships and nurturing key relationships fosters innovation, expands market reach, and mitigates risks.

Competitive Advantage:

A sustainable competitive advantage is essential for distinguishing a business from its rivals and securing its position in the market. This could be achieved through product differentiation, pricing strategies, operational excellence, brand reputation, or proprietary technology.

THE IMPORTANCE OF BUSINESS MODELS IN ENTREPRENEURSHIP

Entrepreneurship is driven by innovation, risk-taking, and the pursuit of opportunity. At the heart of every successful entrepreneurial venture lies a well-crafted business model that serves as the blueprint for converting ideas into sustainable businesses. Understanding the significance of business models in entrepreneurship is crucial for aspiring founders and seasoned entrepreneurs alike.

Strategic Direction:

A business model provides a roadmap for entrepreneurs, guiding them in defining their vision, mission, and strategic objectives. By clearly articulating how the venture will create, deliver, and capture value, entrepreneurs can align their efforts and resources towards achieving long-term goals.

Value Creation:

Business models are designed to create value for both customers and stakeholders. By identifying unmet needs or inefficiencies in the market, entrepreneurs can develop innovative solutions that address these challenges effectively. A compelling value proposition forms the foundation of a successful business model, attracting customers and driving demand for products or services.

Resource Allocation:

Entrepreneurs often face resource constraints, including limited capital, time, and talent. A well-defined business model helps in prioritizing resource allocation, ensuring that scarce resources are utilized efficiently to maximize returns. By focusing on key activities, partnerships, and revenue streams, entrepreneurs can optimize their operations and achieve sustainable growth.

Risk Management:

Entrepreneurship inherently involves risk, but a robust business model helps in mitigating potential risks and uncertainties. By conducting thorough market research, identifying potential challenges, and testing assumptions, entrepreneurs can make informed decisions and adapt their strategies accordingly. Flexibility and resilience built into the business model enable entrepreneurs to navigate unforeseen obstacles and capitalize on emerging opportunities.

Investor Confidence:

Investors and stakeholders often evaluate entrepreneurial ventures based on the strength of their business models. A well-articulated business model demonstrates the entrepreneur's understanding of the market, the viability of the venture, and the potential for scalability and profitability. By instilling confidence in investors, entrepreneurs can secure funding, strategic partnerships, and support for growth initiatives.

Innovation and Adaptation:

In today's rapidly evolving business landscape, innovation and adaptation are essential for staying competitive. A dynamic business model encourages continuous experimentation, iteration, and improvement. By embracing change and harnessing emerging technologies and trends, entrepreneurs can differentiate their offerings, capture new markets, and sustain long-term success.

Scalability and Growth:

Scalability is a key consideration for entrepreneurs looking to expand their ventures and reach new markets. A scalable business model enables entrepreneurs to grow their operations without proportional increases in costs or complexity. By leveraging economies of scale, automation, and strategic partnerships, entrepreneurs can unlock new growth opportunities and maximize their impact.

CHAPTER 2.

THE FOUNDATIONS OF BUSINESS MODEL DEVELOPMENT

The fundamentals of business model creation include recognizing market opportunities, creating value propositions, and analyzing client groups. To build long-term value and income, it is necessary to identify unmet requirements, provide attractive solutions, and target certain client groups.

IDENTIFYING MARKETING OPPORTUNITIES

Identifying market opportunities is an important stage in the development of a successful company model. It entails examining market trends, consumer wants, and competition dynamics to determine where there is a need for new goods or services. Entrepreneurs may offer creative solutions that solve unmet requirements while also adding value to customers by finding and capitalizing on these possibilities. Here are some important ways for discovering market opportunities.

Market Research:
Conducting market research is crucial for understanding industry trends, customer behavior, and the competitive environment. This includes acquiring information from both primary and secondary sources, such as industry publications, consumer surveys, and competition analysis. Entrepreneurs might discover new innovation possibilities by examining market trends and discovering gaps or inefficiencies.

Customer Need Analysis:
Analyzing client wants and pain areas is critical for discovering market prospects. Entrepreneurs should do surveys, interviews, and focus groups with potential clients to learn about their preferences, issues, and unmet requirements. Entrepreneurs may successfully fulfill client demands by recognizing market gaps and understanding the issues they face.

Emerging Trends and Technologies:
Understanding upcoming trends and technology can lead to new market opportunities. Entrepreneurs should be aware of events that may have an influence on their sector, such as technological improvements, changes in customer behaviour, or adjustments in regulatory regimes. Identifying emerging trends early on allows entrepreneurs to capitalize on new possibilities and acquire a competitive advantage.

Industrial Analysis:
Analyzing the competitive environment and market dynamics may help entrepreneurs uncover opportunities for differentiation and development. This includes examining rivals' strengths and weaknesses, as well as spotting market gaps that have previously been missed or underserved. By understanding the competitive landscape, entrepreneurs can identify niches where they can carve out a unique position and capture market share.

Problem-Solving Approach:

Entrepreneurship focuses on solving challenges and meeting unmet needs. Entrepreneurs should develop a problem-solving approach and actively search out possibilities to provide value to customers. Entrepreneurs may offer unique solutions to market pain points and inefficiencies by recognizing them and providing concrete advantages to customers.

DEFINING VALUE PROPOSITIONS

A value proposition is an essential component of every business model because it expresses the distinct advantage or solution that a product or service provides to clients. It is the promise of value that a company makes to its target audience, setting it apart from competitors and driving buyers to pick its products. Defining a great value offer is critical for recruiting and retaining clients, generating revenue growth, and building a sustainable competitive advantage. Here are key considerations for defining value propositions:

Customer Centric Approach:

To create a successful value offer, it's crucial to first identify the wants, preferences, and pain points of your target audience. Entrepreneurs should undertake market research and client interviews to better understand what motivates their target consumers and the issues they want to solve. Understanding the customer's point of view allows entrepreneurs to adjust their value offer to appeal to their target demographic.

Differentiation:
A clear value proposition differentiates a product or service from competitors in the market. Entrepreneurs should find the distinct qualities, benefits, or characteristics that distinguish their services and present them as superior choices. Whether it's through breakthrough technology, great quality, or exceptional customer service, uniqueness is essential for distinguishing out in a competitive market.

Clear and Compelling Messaging:

A value proposition should be communicated in clear, concise language that resonates with the target audience. Entrepreneurs should avoid jargon or technical language and focus on communicating the benefits of their offerings in a way that is easy for customers to understand and relate to. A compelling value proposition should address the customer's pain points and demonstrate how the product or service can solve their problems or improve their lives.

Tangible Benefits:

Customers are motivated by the benefits that a product or service provides, whether it's saving time, saving money, improving productivity, or enhancing quality of life. A strong value proposition clearly communicates the tangible benefits that customers will experience by using the product or service. Entrepreneurs should focus on highlighting the value that their offerings deliver and how they can address the specific needs and desires of their target audience.

Consistency and Authenticity:

Consistency and authenticity are essential for building trust and credibility with customers. A value proposition should accurately reflect the capabilities and qualities of the product or service, and entrepreneurs should strive to deliver on their promises consistently. Authenticity is key to building lasting relationships with customers and fostering loyalty to the brand.

UNDERSTANDING CUSTOMER SEGMENTS

Customer segmentation is a strategic process of dividing a target market into distinct groups of customers with similar characteristics, needs, and behaviors. By understanding customer segments, businesses can tailor their products, services, and marketing strategies to better meet the specific needs and preferences of different customer groups. Here are key considerations for understanding customer segments:

Demographic Segmentation:

Demographic segmentation involves dividing the market based on demographic factors such as age, gender, income, education, occupation, and marital status. These demographic variables provide valuable insights into the characteristics and preferences of different customer groups, allowing businesses to tailor their offerings accordingly.

Psychographic Segmentation:

Psychographic segmentation focuses on dividing the market based on psychographic variables such as attitudes, values, lifestyles, and personality traits. By understanding the psychographic profiles of their target customers, businesses can identify common interests, beliefs, and motivations, enabling them to create more targeted and relevant marketing messages.

Behavioral Segmentation:

Behavioral segmentation involves dividing the market based on customers' behaviors, such as purchase history, usage patterns, brand loyalty, and buying frequency. By analyzing customer behaviors, businesses can identify trends and patterns that indicate different levels of interest, engagement, and loyalty among different customer segments.

Geographic Segmentation:

Geographic segmentation divides the market based on geographic variables such as location, region, climate, and population density. This segmentation strategy is especially useful for firms that sell products or services with regional variances in demand or cultural preferences. Understanding the geographic dispersion of their target market allows firms to customize their marketing strategy to better reach and engage clients in certain regions.

Needs-Based Segmentation:

Needs-based segmentation divides markets based on client needs, preferences, and purchasing reasons. Businesses may create more successful products and services by knowing the individual wants and pain points of different client segments. This method allows firms to differentiate themselves in the market and provide value to customers.

Targeting and Positioning:

After identifying consumer categories, firms may create focused marketing strategies to efficiently reach and engage each category. This entails determining the most appealing categories to target based on characteristics including size, growth potential, and competition intensity. Businesses may then position their products or services in a way that speaks to each segment's specific requirements and preferences, adding value and difference to the marketplace.

In conclusion, knowing customer groups is critical for firms that want to successfully target and engage their target market. Businesses may better address the requirements and preferences of different client segments by categorizing the market based on demographic, psychographic, behavioural, geographic, and needs-based criteria.

CHAPTER 3.

TYPE OF BUSINESS MODELS

Business models vary greatly based on the sector, target market, and value proposition of the company. Some popular types of business models are:

Traditional business models include retail, wholesale, manufacturing, and service-based firms, which create money via the selling of products or services.

Innovative and disruptive models use new technology or business techniques to disrupt conventional sectors and generate new market possibilities. Examples include subscription-based businesses, sharing economy platforms, and on-demand services.

Subscription-Based Models: In these models, users pay a recurring price for access to a product or service over a certain time period. This may include subscription boxes, software-as-a-service (SaaS), and streaming services.

Freemium models provide a free basic version of a product or service, with the opportunity to pay for a premium version with more features or capability. This paradigm is widely adopted in the software, gaming, and media sectors.

Platform models link buyers and sellers and simplify user transactions. Examples include e-commerce marketplaces, social networking platforms, and peer-to-peer lending networks.

These are only a few examples of the various types of business models that exist. The best appropriate model for a certain firm will be determined by its value proposition, target market, and competitive landscape.

TRADITIONAL BUSINESS MODELS

Traditional business models represent the foundational structures upon which many businesses have operated for centuries. While they may vary in specifics across industries, they typically involve the production or distribution of goods and services in exchange for monetary compensation. Here's a detailed exploration of traditional business models:

Retail Business Model:

Retail businesses purchase goods from manufacturers or wholesalers and sell them directly to consumers at a markup. This model often involves physical storefronts, though e-commerce has become increasingly prevalent. Retailers focus on factors like location, product selection, pricing, and customer experience to attract and retain customers.

Wholesale Business Model:

Wholesale businesses buy goods in bulk from manufacturers and sell them in smaller quantities to retailers or other businesses. They typically operate on lower margins but higher volumes compared to retailers. Wholesalers play a crucial role in the supply chain, facilitating the distribution of goods to retailers and ultimately consumers.

Manufacturing Business Model:

Manufacturing businesses produce goods through various processes, including fabrication, assembly, or processing raw materials. They may sell products directly to consumers, businesses, or wholesalers. Manufacturing businesses must manage production processes efficiently to control costs, ensure quality, and meet customer demand.

Service-Based Business Model:

Service-based businesses offer intangible services to clients in exchange for payment. These services can range from consulting and professional services to hospitality and healthcare. Service-based businesses often rely on skilled professionals and expertise to deliver value to clients and maintain a competitive edge.

Brick-and-Mortar Business Model:

Brick-and-mortar businesses operate physical locations where customers can purchase goods or services. These establishments may include retail stores, restaurants, banks, and healthcare facilities. Brick-and-mortar businesses focus on creating welcoming environments, providing convenient access, and offering personalized customer service to attract and retain customers.

Franchise Business Model:

Franchise businesses allow individuals or investors to purchase the rights to operate a business under an established brand name and business model. Franchisors provide training, support, and marketing assistance to franchisees in exchange for ongoing fees or royalties. Franchise models offer entrepreneurs the opportunity to own and operate businesses with reduced risk and access to established brand recognition.

Direct Sales Business Model:

Direct sales businesses sell products directly to consumers through independent representatives or distributors. These representatives typically earn commissions on sales and may recruit and train others to join the sales network. Direct sales models leverage personal relationships, word-of-mouth marketing, and social selling to reach customers and drive sales.

INNOVATIVE AND DISRUPTIVE BUSINESS MODELS

Innovation is the lifeblood of entrepreneurship, driving the creation of new products, services, and business models that challenge the status quo and revolutionize industries. Innovative and disruptive business models represent a departure from traditional approaches, leveraging technology, changing consumer behaviors, and shifting market dynamics to create new opportunities and value propositions. Here's a detailed exploration of these models:

Subscription-Based Models:

Subscription-based models offer customers access to products or services for a recurring fee, typically on a monthly or annual basis. Examples include subscription boxes, streaming services, and software-as-a-service (SaaS) platforms. These models provide recurring revenue streams, foster customer loyalty, and encourage long-term relationships with subscribers.

Sharing Economy Models:

Sharing economy models enable individuals to share resources, goods, or services directly with others, often facilitated by online platforms. Examples include ride-sharing services, peer-to-peer accommodation rentals, and coworking spaces. Sharing economy models promote resource efficiency, cost savings, and community building by leveraging underutilized assets and connecting individuals with mutual needs.

On-Demand Service Models:

On-demand service models provide customers with immediate access to goods or services through digital platforms. Examples include food delivery services, ride-hailing apps, and task-based freelance platforms. These models prioritize convenience, flexibility, and instant gratification, catering to consumers' desire for seamless, frictionless experiences.

Freemium Models:

Freemium models offer a basic version of a product or service for free, with optional premium features or content available for a fee. Examples include freemium mobile apps, software with limited functionality, and online content platforms. Freemium models lower barriers to entry, drive user acquisition, and monetize customer engagement through upselling and cross-selling opportunities.

Platform-Based Models:

Platform-based models facilitate transactions, interactions, or exchanges between multiple parties through digital platforms. Examples include e-commerce marketplaces, social media networks, and crowd funding platforms. Platform models create value by connecting buyers and sellers, fostering network effects, and leveraging data to personalize user experiences.

Direct-to-Consumer (DTC) Models:

Direct-to-consumer models enable brands to sell products directly to customers without intermediaries like retailers or wholesalers. Examples include DTC apparel brands, subscription meal kits, and online eyewear retailers. DTC models offer greater control over the customer experience, enable data-driven marketing, and allow brands to capture higher margins.

Blockchain-Based Models:

Blockchain-based models leverage decentralized, transparent, and secure ledger technology to facilitate peer-to-peer transactions, contracts, or agreements. Examples include cryptocurrencies, smart contracts, and decentralized finance (DeFi) platforms. Blockchain models promise greater trust, security, and efficiency by eliminating intermediaries and reducing transaction costs.

SUBSCRIPTION-BASED MODELS

Subscription-based models have gained significant traction across various industries, offering customers access to products or services in exchange for recurring payments. From entertainment and software to healthcare and education, subscription-based models provide businesses with predictable revenue streams while offering consumers convenience, flexibility, and value. Here's a detailed exploration of subscription-based models:

Types of Subscription-Based Models:

Product Subscriptions: Customers receive physical products on a recurring basis, such as subscription boxes for cosmetics, meal kits, or clothing.

Service Subscriptions: Customers access ongoing services for a recurring fee, such as streaming platforms for music, movies, or fitness classes.

Membership Subscriptions: Customers gain access to exclusive benefits, perks, or content, such as subscription-based loyalty programs or premium memberships.

Benefits for Businesses:

Predictable Revenue: Subscription-based models provide businesses with steady, predictable revenue streams, making it easier to forecast finances and plan for growth.

Customer Retention: Subscriptions encourage long-term customer relationships, fostering loyalty and reducing churn through recurring engagement.

Upselling and Cross-Selling: Businesses can upsell or cross-sell additional products or services to subscribers, increasing average revenue per user (ARPU) over time.

Data-Driven Insights: Subscription models generate valuable data on customer preferences, behaviors, and usage patterns, enabling businesses to personalize offerings and optimize marketing strategies.

Benefits for Consumers:

Convenience: Subscriptions offer consumers hassle-free access to products or services without the need for repeated transactions or commitments.

Cost Savings: Subscribers often receive discounted rates or bundled packages, providing value and cost savings compared to one-time purchases.

Customization: Subscription services may offer personalized recommendations, curated content, or customizable options based on individual preferences.

Flexibility: Many subscription-based models allow consumers to adjust or cancel their subscriptions easily, providing flexibility to accommodate changing needs or circumstances.

Key Considerations for Success:

Value Proposition: Businesses must offer compelling value propositions that resonate with customers and justify the recurring investment.

Retention Strategies: Retaining subscribers is critical for long-term success, requiring businesses to deliver consistent quality, engage customers, and address feedback promptly.

Customer Acquisition: Effective marketing and customer acquisition strategies are essential for attracting new subscribers and growing the subscriber base.

Pricing Strategy: Businesses must carefully consider pricing structures, balancing affordability with profitability and perceived value to maximize subscription uptake.

Examples of Successful Subscription-Based Models:

Netflix: A leading streaming platform offering a wide range of movies, TV shows, and original content on a monthly subscription basis.

Amazon Prime: A membership program providing subscribers with benefits such as free two-day shipping, streaming services, and exclusive deals.

Dollar Shave Club: A subscription-based service delivering razors and grooming products directly to customers' doors on a recurring basis.

In summary, subscription-based models continue to redefine how businesses engage with customers, offering mutually beneficial arrangements that provide convenience, value, and recurring revenue. Whether in entertainment, retail, software, or beyond, subscription models offer a compelling proposition for businesses and consumers alike, driving innovation and reshaping industries in the digital age.

CHAPTER 4.

DESIGNING YOUR BUSINESS MODEL CANVAS

Designing your business model canvas is a strategic exercise that involves visualizing and organizing key elements of your business model onto a single, concise framework. The business model canvas, popularized by Alexander Osterwalder, consists of nine building blocks: customer segments, value proposition, channels, customer relationships, revenue streams, key resources, key activities, key partnerships, and cost structure. By systematically mapping out these elements, entrepreneurs can gain clarity on how their business creates, delivers, and captures value, facilitating better decision-making and strategic planning.

KEY ELEMENTS AND COMPONENTS OF A BUSINESS MODEL CANVAS

The business model canvas is a strategic tool used by entrepreneurs and businesses to visualize and design their business models. It consists of nine key elements or building blocks that capture the essential aspects of a business. Understanding these elements and their interrelationships is crucial for developing a comprehensive and effective business model. Here's a detailed exploration of each key element:

Customer Segments:

Customer segments identify the different groups of customers or users that a business serves. These segments may be based on demographics, psychographics, behaviors, or other characteristics.

Understanding customer segments helps businesses tailor their products, services, and marketing strategies to meet the specific needs and preferences of different customer groups.

Value Proposition:

The value proposition articulates the unique benefits or solutions that a business offers to its customers. It describes why customers should choose the business over competitors and how it addresses their needs or solves their problems.

A compelling value proposition is essential for attracting and retaining customers, differentiating the business from competitors, and creating value in the marketplace.

Channels:

Channels represent the various ways in which a business reaches and interacts with its customers to deliver its value proposition. These channels may include physical storefronts, online platforms, direct sales teams, or distribution partners.

Choosing the right channels enables businesses to effectively reach their target customers, deliver value, and facilitate transactions or interactions.

Customer Relationships:

Customer relationships describe the types of interactions and engagements that a business has with its customers throughout the customer lifecycle. These relationships may range from personal to automated, depending on the nature of the business and its customers.

Cultivating strong customer relationships is essential for building trust, loyalty, and repeat business, as well as for gathering feedback and insights to improve the customer experience.

Revenue Streams:

Revenue streams represent the sources of revenue for a business, derived from the sale of products, services, or other offerings to customers. These streams may include one-time sales, recurring subscriptions, licensing fees, or advertising revenue.

Diversifying revenue streams helps businesses reduce risk, maximize revenue potential, and capture value from different customer segments or channels.

Key Resources:

Key resources are the assets, capabilities, and infrastructure that a business requires to deliver its value proposition, operate its activities, and generate revenue. These resources may include physical, human, financial, or intellectual assets.

Identifying and leveraging key resources enables businesses to build competitive advantages, scale operations, and sustain long-term growth.

Key Activities:

Key activities are the core functions and processes that a business performs to deliver its value proposition and operate its business model effectively. These activities may include product development, manufacturing, marketing, sales, customer support, and logistics.

Focusing on key activities helps businesses allocate resources efficiently, streamline operations, and prioritize efforts that drive value creation and competitive advantage.

Key Partnerships:

Key partnerships involve collaborations with other businesses, organizations, or stakeholders that contribute to the success of the business model.

These partnerships may include suppliers, distributors, technology providers, or strategic alliances.

Forming and managing key partnerships enables businesses to access resources, capabilities, and expertise that complement their own, accelerate growth, and mitigate risks.

Cost Structure:

The cost structure outlines the expenses and investments that a business incurs in operating its business model and delivering its value proposition. These costs may include fixed costs, variable costs, and one-time expenses.

Understanding the cost structure helps businesses manage costs effectively, optimize resource allocation, and maintain profitability while delivering value to customers.

PRACTICAL APPLICATION EXAMPLES OF BUSINESS MODEL CANVAS

The business model canvas is a versatile tool that can be applied to various industries and businesses, providing a structured framework for analyzing, designing, and iterating on business models. Here are some practical application examples of how businesses have used the business model canvas:

Startup Ventures:

Startup founders often use the business model canvas to conceptualize and refine their business ideas. By mapping out key elements such as customer segments, value proposition, and revenue streams, entrepreneurs can validate assumptions, identify potential risks, and develop strategies for growth.

Existing Businesses:

Established businesses can use the business model canvas to evaluate and optimize their existing business models. By assessing current strategies, identifying areas for improvement, and exploring new opportunities, businesses can adapt to changing market conditions, innovate, and remain competitive.

Product Development:

Product development teams can use the business model canvas to align product features and functionalities with customer needs and market opportunities. By focusing on key elements such as value proposition, customer segments, and channels, teams can ensure that products are well-positioned to meet market demand and generate revenue.

Marketing and Sales Strategies:

Marketing and sales teams can use the business model canvas to develop targeted strategies for reaching and engaging customers. By understanding customer segments, channels, and value propositions, teams can tailor messaging, promotions, and distribution tactics to maximize customer acquisition and retention.

Strategic Planning:

Business leaders can use the business model canvas to inform strategic decision-making and long-term planning. By analyzing key elements such as revenue streams, cost structure, and key resources, leaders can assess the viability of different growth opportunities, allocate resources effectively, and chart a course for sustainable success.

Partnership Development:

Businesses can use the business model canvas to identify potential partners and collaborations that enhance their business models. By evaluating key partnerships, resources, and activities, businesses can leverage complementary strengths, access new markets, and drive innovation through strategic alliances.

Innovation and Iteration:

The business model canvas encourages experimentation, iteration, and innovation. Businesses can use the canvas to test new ideas, pivot in response to market feedback, and refine their business models over time. By continuously assessing and adapting key elements, businesses can stay agile, responsive, and resilient in dynamic market environments.

Entrepreneurial Education:

Educators and entrepreneurship programs use the business model canvas to teach students about business fundamentals and entrepreneurial thinking. By engaging with real-world examples and case studies, students can apply the canvas to analyze business models, develop business plans, and explore entrepreneurship opportunities.

In summary, the business model canvas offers a practical and adaptable framework for businesses of all sizes and industries to analyze, design, and optimize their business models. By applying the canvas in various contexts—from startup ventures to strategic planning and partnership development—businesses can gain insights, drive innovation, and create value in the marketplace.

CHAPTER 5.

REVENUE STREAMS AND PRICING STRATEGIES

Revenue streams and pricing strategies are crucial components of any business model. Revenue streams represent the sources of income for a business, while pricing strategies determine how products or services are priced and sold to customers. By identifying diverse revenue streams and implementing effective pricing strategies, businesses can optimize revenue generation, maximize profitability, and create sustainable business models.

MONETIZATION MODELS: EXPLORING REVENUE STRATEGIES

Monetization models represent the strategies businesses use to generate revenue from their products, services, or platforms. These models are fundamental to the sustainability and profitability of a business, as they determine how value is exchanged between the business and its customers or users. Here's a detailed exploration of various monetization models:

Advertising:

Advertising monetization involves displaying advertisements to users and generating revenue through ad impressions, clicks, or conversions. This model is commonly used in media, publishing, and digital platforms, where advertisers pay to reach target audiences.

Subscription:

Subscription monetization offers customers access to products or services in exchange for recurring payments. This model is prevalent in industries such as software, media streaming, and membership-based services, providing businesses with predictable revenue streams and fostering customer loyalty.

Transaction Fees:

Transaction fee monetization involves charging a fee for facilitating transactions between buyers and sellers. This model is common in e-commerce, online marketplaces, and payment processing platforms, where businesses earn revenue by facilitating transactions and processing payments.

Freemium:

Freemium monetization offers a basic version of a product or service for free, with optional premium features or content available for a fee. This model encourages user adoption and engagement while monetizing premium offerings, such as additional features, content, or functionality.

Licensing and Royalties:

Licensing and royalties monetization involves licensing intellectual property, such as patents, trademarks, or copyrights, to third parties in exchange for royalties or licensing fees. This model is prevalent in industries such as technology, entertainment, and franchising, where businesses monetize their intellectual assets.

Affiliate Marketing:

Affiliate marketing monetization involves earning commissions by promoting third-party products or services and driving sales or referrals through affiliate links or partnerships. This model is common in e-commerce, digital marketing, and content publishing, where businesses earn revenue through performance-based marketing efforts.

Sponsorship:

Sponsorship monetization involves partnering with sponsors or advertisers to fund products, events, or content in exchange for brand exposure and visibility. This model is prevalent in sports, entertainment, and media industries, where businesses monetize their audience or content through sponsorship deals.

Data Monetization:

Data monetization involves leveraging data assets, such as user data, insights, or analytics, to generate revenue through targeted advertising, market research, or data licensing. This model is common in digital platforms, social media, and technology companies, where data is a valuable asset for monetization.

PRICING TACTICS AND STRATEGIES: MAXIMIZING REVENUE AND VALUE

Pricing tactics and strategies are essential components of a business's revenue strategy, influencing customer perception, purchasing decisions, and overall profitability. By employing effective pricing tactics and strategies, businesses can optimize revenue generation, capture value, and maintain a competitive edge in the marketplace. Here's a detailed exploration of various pricing tactics and strategies:

Cost-Based Pricing:

Cost-based pricing involves setting prices based on the costs of production, distribution, and overhead, with a desired profit margin added on top. This approach ensures that prices cover costs and generate profit, but may not reflect market demand or customer willingness to pay.

Value-Based Pricing:

Value-based pricing focuses on the perceived value of a product or service to customers, rather than its production costs. This approach considers factors such as customer benefits, competitive alternatives, and willingness to pay, allowing businesses to capture maximum value and justify premium prices.

Competitive Pricing:

Competitive pricing involves setting prices based on competitors' prices, market trends, and industry benchmarks. This approach aims to position prices competitively within the market while maintaining profitability and market share relative to competitors.

Dynamic Pricing:

Dynamic pricing adjusts prices in real-time based on factors such as demand, supply, seasonality, and customer behavior. This approach allows businesses to optimize prices dynamically to maximize revenue, capture value, and respond to market fluctuations and changes in demand.

Price Discrimination:

Price discrimination involves charging different prices to different customer segments based on their willingness to pay, preferences, or purchasing power. This tactic allows businesses to capture additional value from different customer groups while optimizing revenue and maximizing profitability.

Bundle Pricing:

Bundle pricing combines multiple products or services into a single package and offers them at a discounted price compared to purchasing items individually. This tactic encourages upselling, increases perceived value, and stimulates demand by offering savings to customers.

Freemium Pricing:

Freemium pricing offers a basic version of a product or service for free, with premium features or content available for a fee. This tactic encourages user adoption, builds a user base, and monetizes premium offerings, such as additional features, functionality, or content.

Psychological Pricing:

Psychological pricing leverages human psychology and cognitive biases to influence perception and purchasing decisions. Tactics such as charm pricing (e.g., pricing products at $9.99 instead of $10) and decoy pricing (e.g., offering a premium option to make other options seem more attractive) can influence customer behavior and increase sales.

In conclusion, pricing tactics and strategies are powerful tools for businesses to optimize revenue, capture value, and remain competitive in the marketplace. By understanding customer needs, market dynamics, and competitive pressures, businesses can implement effective pricing strategies that maximize profitability while delivering value to customers.

CHAPTER 6.

BUILDING SUSTAINABLE COMPETITIVE ADVANTAGE

Building sustainable competitive advantage is essential for long-term success in business. It involves creating unique strengths or assets that competitors cannot easily replicate, allowing a business to outperform rivals and maintain market leadership over time. By focusing on innovation, customer relationships, operational excellence, or other strategic pillars, businesses can differentiate themselves, create value for customers, and achieve sustainable growth in the marketplace.

DIFFERENTIATION STRATEGIES: CREATING VALUE AND COMPETITIVE ADVANTAGE

Differentiation strategies are fundamental to establishing a competitive edge in the marketplace by offering unique and distinct attributes that set a business apart from competitors. By focusing on innovation, quality, customer experience, or other value drivers, businesses can differentiate their products or services to attract customers, command premium prices, and build brand loyalty. Here's a detailed exploration of various differentiation strategies:

Product Differentiation:

Product differentiation involves offering products with unique features, performance, or design that distinguish them from competitors' offerings. This may include innovations in technology, design, functionality, or packaging that enhance value and meet specific customer needs or preferences.

Service Differentiation:

Service differentiation focuses on delivering superior customer service, support, or experiences that exceed customer expectations and enhance satisfaction. This may include personalized service, prompt responsiveness, hassle-free returns, or exclusive benefits that differentiate the business in the eyes of customers.

Brand Differentiation:

Brand differentiation revolves around building a strong brand identity, reputation, and emotional connection with customers that sets the business apart from competitors. This may include unique brand positioning, messaging, values, or associations that resonate with target customers and foster brand loyalty.

Pricing Differentiation:

Pricing differentiation involves offering products or services at different price points or with different pricing structures to appeal to different customer segments or market segments. This may include premium pricing for high-end offerings, value pricing for budget-conscious customers, or dynamic pricing based on demand.

Distribution Differentiation:

Distribution differentiation focuses on offering unique distribution channels, locations, or partnerships that provide customers with convenient access to products or services. This may include exclusive partnerships, online platforms, or innovative delivery options that enhance accessibility and reach new customer segments.

Innovation Differentiation:

Innovation differentiation involves continuous innovation and improvement to stay ahead of competitors and meet evolving customer needs. This may include product innovation, process innovation, business model innovation, or technological innovation that drives value creation and differentiation.

Quality Differentiation:

Quality differentiation emphasizes delivering superior quality products or services that exceed industry standards and meet or exceed customer expectations. This may include rigorous quality control, certifications, warranties, or guarantees that reinforce the business's commitment to excellence and customer satisfaction.

Experience Differentiation:

Experience differentiation focuses on creating memorable and positive customer experiences across all touchpoints, from pre-purchase to post-purchase interactions. This may include intuitive user interfaces, engaging marketing campaigns, seamless transactions, and personalized recommendations that delight customers and build brand loyalty.

CREATING BARRIERS TO ENTRY: SECURING COMPETITIVE ADVANTAGE

In business, creating barriers to entry is essential for establishing a competitive advantage and protecting market position from new entrants.

Barriers to entry are factors or conditions that make it difficult for new competitors to enter an industry or market and compete effectively. By strategically implementing barriers to entry, businesses can deter competition, maintain market share, and sustain profitability over the long term. Here's a detailed exploration of how businesses can create barriers to entry:

Economies of Scale:

Economies of scale arise when businesses can produce goods or services at lower average costs as production volume increases. By achieving economies of scale through efficient production, distribution, or operations, businesses can lower costs and price competitively, making it challenging for new entrants to compete on cost.

Brand Loyalty and Reputation:

Strong brand loyalty and reputation can serve as significant barriers to entry, as customers may be reluctant to switch to new or unknown brands. By building a trusted brand identity, delivering consistent quality and value, and cultivating loyal customer relationships, businesses can protect market share and deter competitors.

Intellectual Property Protection:

Intellectual property protection, such as patents, trademarks, and copyrights, can create legal barriers to entry by preventing competitors from copying or replicating proprietary technologies, designs, or content. By securing intellectual property rights and enforcing them rigorously, businesses can safeguard their innovations and maintain a competitive edge.

Regulatory Compliance and Licensing:

Regulatory compliance requirements and licensing barriers can deter new entrants by imposing significant costs, time, and complexity on businesses seeking to enter regulated industries or markets. By navigating regulatory hurdles, obtaining necessary licenses, and complying with industry standards, businesses can create barriers to entry and maintain market exclusivity.

High Capital Requirements:

High capital requirements, such as significant upfront investments in equipment, infrastructure, or technology, can deter new entrants by raising the barriers to entry. By investing in capital-intensive assets and resources, businesses can establish cost advantages and economies of scale that new competitors may find challenging to match.

Access to Distribution Channels:

Access to established distribution channels, networks, or partnerships can create barriers to entry by limiting new entrants' ability to reach customers effectively. By building strategic relationships with distributors, retailers, or intermediaries, businesses can control access to distribution channels and maintain market dominance.

Switching Costs:

Switching costs refer to the costs or inconvenience associated with switching from one product, service, or supplier to another. By creating high switching costs through contractual agreements, proprietary technologies, or lock-in mechanisms, businesses can discourage customers from switching to competitors and protect market share.

Network Effects:

Network effects occur when the value of a product or service increases as more users adopt it, creating a barrier to entry for new competitors. By building large user bases, fostering user engagement, and leveraging network effects, businesses can establish strong competitive advantages and monopolize markets.

In conclusion, creating barriers to entry is essential for businesses seeking to establish competitive advantage, protect market share, and sustain profitability in dynamic and competitive markets. By strategically leveraging factors such as economies of scale, brand loyalty, intellectual property protection, and regulatory compliance, businesses can deter competition, maintain market dominance, and achieve long-term success.

CHAPTER 7.

SCALING AND GROWTH STRATEGIES

Scaling and growth strategies are essential for businesses aiming to expand their operations, reach new markets, and increase profitability. These strategies involve increasing production, expanding distribution channels, entering new markets, or acquiring competitors to achieve sustainable growth and competitive advantage. By implementing effective scaling and growth strategies, businesses can capitalize on opportunities, optimize resources, and achieve their long-term objectives.

EXPANDING YOUR MARKET REACH

Expanding your market reach is essential for businesses seeking to grow their customer base, increase sales, and maximize profitability. By reaching new markets, businesses can tap into additional revenue streams, diversify their customer base, and reduce dependence on existing markets. Here's some valuable information on expanding your market reach:

Market Research:

Conduct thorough market research to identify potential target markets, understand customer needs and preferences, and assess competition. Analyze demographic data, market trends, and consumer behavior to uncover opportunities for expansion.

Product or Service Adaptation:

Adapt your products or services to meet the unique needs and preferences of new target markets. Customize offerings, features, or pricing strategies to align with local market demands and preferences, ensuring relevance and appeal to new customers.

Distribution Channels:

Explore new distribution channels or partnerships to reach customers in different geographic regions or market segments. Consider online platforms, retail outlets, distributors, or strategic alliances to expand your reach and increase accessibility to customers.

Marketing and Promotion:

Develop targeted marketing and promotion strategies to raise awareness and attract customers in new markets. Tailor messaging, advertising campaigns, and promotional activities to resonate with local audiences and communicate the value proposition effectively.

Digital Presence:

Strengthen your digital presence to extend your market reach and engage with customers across different channels and platforms. Invest in website optimization, search engine marketing, social media, and online advertising to expand your online visibility and reach new audiences.

Localization and Cultural Sensitivity:

Consider cultural nuances, language preferences, and local customs when expanding into new markets. Adapt marketing materials, communication strategies, and product offerings to reflect cultural diversity and foster connection with local customers.

Customer Support and Service:

Provide excellent customer support and service to build trust, loyalty, and satisfaction among new customers. Offer responsive communication channels, personalized assistance, and after-sales support to address customer inquiries and resolve issues effectively.

Monitor and Adapt:

Continuously monitor market dynamics, customer feedback and performance metrics to assess the effectiveness of your expansion efforts. Adapt strategies, refine tactics, and iterate based on insights and feedback to optimize market reach and drive sustainable growth.

Expanding your market reach requires careful planning, strategic execution, and ongoing evaluation to identify opportunities, mitigate risks, and achieve success in new markets. By leveraging market insights, adapting offerings, and deploying targeted marketing strategies, businesses can extend their reach, attract new customers, and unlock growth opportunities in diverse markets.

MANAGING GROWTH CHALLENGES

Managing growth challenges is a crucial aspect of navigating the complexities that come with expanding a business. While growth is often desirable, it also presents various challenges that can strain resources, disrupt operations, and hinder progress if not addressed effectively. Here's some valuable information on managing growth challenges:

Resource Constraints:

Rapid growth can strain resources such as capital, manpower, and infrastructure. To address this challenge, businesses should prioritize resource allocation, invest in scalable systems and technologies, and consider strategic partnerships or outsourcing to meet increased demand efficiently.

Operational Scalability:

Scaling operations to accommodate growth requires careful planning and execution. Businesses should streamline processes, automate repetitive tasks, and implement scalable systems and workflows to maintain efficiency and productivity as operations expand.

Talent Acquisition and Retention:

Finding and retaining skilled employees becomes increasingly challenging during periods of rapid growth. To overcome this challenge, businesses should invest in talent acquisition strategies, offer competitive compensation and benefits, provide opportunities for professional development, and foster a positive workplace culture to attract and retain top talent.

Customer Experience and Satisfaction:

Maintaining high levels of customer satisfaction becomes more challenging as the customer base expands. Businesses should prioritize customer experience, invest in customer support and service, gather feedback proactively, and address issues promptly to ensure customer retention and loyalty amidst growth.

Market Expansion and Diversification:

Expanding into new markets or diversifying product offerings can present challenges such as market saturation, competition, and regulatory hurdles. Businesses should conduct thorough market research, assess market potential and risks, tailor offerings to meet local demand, and adapt strategies based on market feedback to maximize success in new ventures.

Financial Management:

Managing finances becomes more complex as revenue streams increase and expenses grow. Businesses should implement robust financial management practices, monitor cash flow, budget effectively, and seek financing options when necessary to sustain growth and ensure financial stability amidst expansion.

Maintaining Organizational Culture:

Preserving the company's culture and values can become challenging as the organization grows and evolves. Businesses should communicate core values, lead by example, involve employees in decision-making, and foster a sense of belonging and purpose to maintain a strong organizational culture amidst growth.

Risk Management:

Growth introduces new risks and uncertainties that can impact business operations and viability. Businesses should identify potential risks, develop contingency plans, and implement risk mitigation strategies to anticipate and address challenges such as market volatility, supply chain disruptions, regulatory changes, and unforeseen events.

Effectively managing growth challenges requires proactive planning, strategic decision-making, and continuous adaptation to changing circumstances. By addressing resource constraints, optimizing operations, nurturing talent, prioritizing customer satisfaction, and managing risks effectively, businesses can navigate growth challenges successfully and unlock opportunities for sustainable expansion and long-term success.

CHAPTER 8.

BUSINESS MODEL INNOVATION AND ADAPTATION

Business model innovation and adaptation are essential for businesses to stay relevant and competitive in dynamic and evolving markets. By continuously exploring new business models, adapting to changing customer needs, and embracing innovation, businesses can drive growth, create value, and maintain relevance in an ever-changing landscape. Whether through new revenue streams, distribution channels, pricing models, or value propositions, businesses must remain agile and proactive in innovating and adapting their business models to meet the demands of the market and stay ahead of the competition.

RESPONDING TO MARKET CHANGES: STRATEGIES FOR BUSINESS AGILITY

Market changes are inevitable in the dynamic and competitive landscape of business. Whether driven by technological advancements, shifts in consumer preferences, economic fluctuations, or regulatory developments, businesses must adapt swiftly to stay relevant, competitive, and profitable. Here's a detailed exploration of strategies for responding to market changes effectively:

Continuous Monitoring and Analysis:

Stay informed about market trends, industry developments, and competitive landscapes through continuous monitoring and analysis. Utilize market research, data analytics, and competitive intelligence to identify emerging opportunities and threats and anticipate changes in customer needs and market dynamics.

Agile Decision-Making:

Foster a culture of agility and flexibility within the organization to respond quickly and decisively to market changes. Empower employees to make autonomous decisions, streamline decision-making processes, and prioritize speed and adaptability in responding to changing circumstances.

Customer-Centric Approach:

Put the customer at the center of your business strategy and decision-making process. Listen to customer feedback, gather insights through surveys, focus groups, and social media monitoring, and adapt products, services, and experiences to meet evolving customer needs and preferences.

Innovative Product and Service Development:

Invest in innovation and product development to create differentiated offerings that address emerging market trends and customer demands.

Embrace new technologies, explore novel business models, and collaborate with customers, partners, and stakeholders to drive innovation and stay ahead of the competition.

Strategic Partnerships and Alliances:

Forge strategic partnerships and alliances with complementary businesses, suppliers, distributors, or technology providers to leverage collective strengths, access new markets, and mitigate risks associated with market changes. Collaborate on joint ventures, co-marketing initiatives, or co-development projects to capitalize on synergies and expand market reach.

Diversification and Expansion:

Diversify products, services, or markets to reduce reliance on specific segments or geographies and mitigate the impact of market changes. Explore new growth opportunities, enter adjacent markets, or expand into emerging industries to diversify revenue streams and capitalize on evolving market trends.

Operational Efficiency and Cost Optimization:

Streamline operations, improve efficiency, and optimize costs to enhance agility and flexibility in responding to market changes. Adopt lean practices, invest in automation and digitalization, and reevaluate resource allocation to ensure optimal use of resources and maximize profitability amidst changing market conditions.

Risk Management and Contingency Planning:

Develop robust risk management strategies and contingency plans to anticipate and mitigate the impact of market changes on business operations. Identify potential risks, assess their likelihood and impact, and implement proactive measures to mitigate risks and ensure business continuity in uncertain environments.

Adaptation and Learning:

Embrace a mindset of continuous learning, adaptation, and experimentation to navigate market changes effectively. Learn from successes and failures, gather feedback, iterate on strategies, and remain open to new ideas and approaches to stay resilient and responsive in dynamic market environments.

Responding to market changes requires proactive planning, strategic foresight, and a willingness to adapt and innovate in the face of uncertainty. By embracing agility, customer-centricity, innovation, and strategic partnerships, businesses can navigate market changes successfully, seize opportunities, and drive sustainable growth and competitiveness in the ever-evolving marketplace.

PIVOTING STRATEGIES: NAVIGATING CHANGE WITH AGILITY

Pivoting strategies are essential for businesses facing challenges or opportunities that require a fundamental change in direction or approach. Whether prompted by shifts in market conditions, customer needs, technology disruptions, or competitive pressures, pivoting enables businesses to adapt, innovate, and thrive in dynamic environments. Here's a detailed exploration of pivoting strategies and their implementation:

Identify Trigger Points:

Recognize key trigger points or indicators that signal the need for a pivot, such as declining sales, changing customer preferences, or disruptive market trends. Stay vigilant for early warning signs and be proactive in assessing the need for change.

Assess Current Situation:

Conduct a comprehensive assessment of your current business model, market positioning, strengths, weaknesses, opportunities, and threats. Evaluate performance metrics, customer feedback, and competitive analysis to identify areas for improvement or potential pivot opportunities.

Define New Direction:

Define a clear vision and strategic direction for the pivot, based on insights gathered from the assessment process. Identify new market opportunities, customer segments, product offerings, or business models that align with your strengths and capitalize on emerging trends.

Experiment and Iterate:

Embrace a culture of experimentation and iteration to test new ideas, concepts, and strategies before committing to a full-scale pivot. Start small, gather feedback, measure results, and iterate based on insights to refine and optimize the pivot strategy over time.

Customer-Centric Approach:

Prioritize the needs, preferences, and feedback of your customers throughout the pivoting process. Engage with customers, gather insights, and involve them in co-creation to ensure that the pivot aligns with their evolving needs and delivers value effectively.

Rapid Prototyping and MVPs:

Develop minimum viable products (MVPs) or prototypes to quickly validate new ideas and concepts with minimal resources and time investment. Gather feedback from early adopters, iterate based on user insights, and refine the product or service iteratively to optimize market fit.

Agile Execution:

Execute the pivot with agility, flexibility, and a bias towards action. Break down the pivot into smaller, manageable tasks, set clear objectives and timelines, and empower cross-functional teams to collaborate and adapt quickly to changing circumstances.

Communicate Effectively:

Communicate the pivot strategy, rationale, and vision clearly and transparently to internal stakeholders, employees, customers, investors, and partners. Engage with stakeholders, address concerns, and build buy-in and alignment around the pivot to ensure support and commitment to its success.

Measure and Monitor Progress:

Establish key performance indicators (KPIs) and metrics to track the progress and success of the pivot. Monitor performance against objectives, gather feedback from stakeholders, and adjust strategies as needed to stay on course and drive desired outcomes.

Iterate and Learn:

Embrace a mindset of continuous learning, adaptation, and iteration throughout the pivoting process. Learn from successes and failures, gather insights, and iterate on strategies based on feedback and market dynamics to optimize outcomes and drive sustainable growth.

Pivoting is a strategic imperative for businesses seeking to navigate change, seize opportunities, and remain competitive in dynamic and uncertain environments. By adopting a customer-centric approach, embracing agility, experimentation, and iteration, and communicating effectively with stakeholders, businesses can execute successful pivots that drive innovation, growth, and resilience in the face of adversity or disruption.

CHAPTER 9.

CASE STUDIES AND REAL-LIFE EXAMPLES

Case studies and real-life examples offer valuable insights and practical learning for businesses seeking inspiration, best practices, and solutions to challenges. By examining real-world scenarios, success stories, and lessons learned from other organizations, businesses can gain valuable perspectives, identify trends, and apply relevant strategies to their own context. Whether it's a successful product launch, a strategic pivot, or a crisis management response, case studies and real-life examples provide tangible evidence of effective strategies, innovative approaches, and impactful outcomes that can inform and inspire business decision-making.

SUCCESSFUL BUSINESS MODEL INNOVATIONS: DRIVING GROWTH AND COMPETITIVE ADVANTAGE

Business model innovations are crucial for organizations seeking to differentiate themselves, create value, and sustain long-term success in dynamic and competitive markets. Successful business model innovations not only disrupt industries but also revolutionize the way businesses operate, deliver value, and capture market share. Here's a detailed exploration of characteristics and examples of successful business model innovations:

Value Proposition Reinvention:

Successful business model innovations often involve reimagining the value proposition to address unmet customer needs or solve persistent pain points in new and innovative ways. Examples include Netflix's shift from DVD rentals to subscription-based streaming services, offering greater convenience and access to content.

Disruptive Technology Adoption:

Embracing disruptive technologies can drive successful business model innovations by enabling new products, services, or distribution channels. For instance, Uber leveraged mobile technology to disrupt the traditional taxi industry by offering on-demand ride-hailing services through a digital platform, revolutionizing transportation.

Platform Ecosystem Creation:

Building platform ecosystems that connect multiple stakeholders and facilitate value exchange can lead to successful business model innovations. Amazon's transformation from an online bookstore to a global e-commerce platform and marketplace enabled third-party sellers to reach customers worldwide, fueling exponential growth and revenue diversification.

Subscription-Based Revenue Models:

Subscription-based revenue models offer predictable revenue streams and foster customer loyalty, driving successful business model innovations. Adobe's transition from selling software licenses to a subscription-based model with Adobe Creative Cloud provided customers with continuous updates and access to a suite of creative tools, enhancing value and recurring revenue.

Freemium and Monetization Strategies:

Freemium models, offering basic services for free with premium features available for a fee, have led to successful business model innovations by attracting users and monetizing premium offerings. Spotify's freemium music streaming model offers ad-supported free access to its platform, while premium subscriptions provide ad-free listening and additional features.

Marketplace and Network Effects:

Building marketplaces that leverage network effects can drive successful business model innovations by connecting buyers and sellers, creating value for both sides. Airbnb disrupted the hospitality industry by creating a platform that connects travelers with hosts offering unique accommodations, leveraging network effects to scale rapidly and expand globally.

Sharing Economy and Asset Light Models:

The sharing economy and asset-light business models have led to successful business model innovations by utilizing existing resources more efficiently. Airbnb and Uber exemplify this approach by leveraging underutilized assets (homes and vehicles) to offer accommodations and transportation services, respectively, without owning physical assets.

Vertical Integration and Value Chain Disruption:

Vertically integrating across the value chain or disrupting traditional value chains can drive successful business model innovations by capturing value and streamlining operations. Tesla's direct-to-consumer sales model bypasses traditional dealership networks, enabling greater control over pricing, customer experience, and distribution.

Successful Business Model Innovations:

Successful business model innovations are characterized by their ability to create value, disrupt industries, and drive sustainable growth and competitive advantage. By embracing customer-centricity, leveraging technology, fostering innovation, and challenging industry norms, organizations can create business models that resonate with customers, capture market share, and redefine industry standards in the pursuit of long-term success.

LESSONS LEARNED FROM FAILURES: NAVIGATING SETBACKS TO DRIVE SUCCESS

Failures are an inevitable part of the business journey, but they also provide invaluable opportunities for learning, growth, and improvement. While failures can be painful and discouraging, they often contain valuable lessons that can inform future decisions, strategies, and actions. Here's a detailed exploration of lessons learned from failures:

Embrace Failure as a Learning Opportunity:

Rather than viewing failure as a setback, embrace it as a learning opportunity. Analyze the root causes of failure, identify key lessons learned, and extract insights that can inform future decision-making and strategy development.

Identify Failure Patterns:

Look for patterns or recurring themes in past failures to identify underlying issues or weaknesses in the business model, strategy, or execution. Understanding common failure patterns can help businesses anticipate and mitigate risks more effectively in the future.

Fail Fast and Iterate:

Embrace a fail-fast mentality that encourages experimentation, iteration, and rapid learning. Instead of dwelling on past failures, iterate on ideas, products, or strategies quickly, gather feedback, and adapt based on insights to drive continuous improvement and innovation.

Foster a Culture of Transparency and Accountability:

Cultivate a culture of transparency, open communication, and accountability within the organization. Encourage employees to share their failures openly, without fear of judgment, and foster a supportive environment where failures are viewed as opportunities for growth and learning.

Encourage Risk-Taking and Innovation:

Encourage calculated risk-taking and experimentation to drive innovation and creativity within the organization. Provide employees with the autonomy and resources to pursue new ideas, test hypotheses, and explore innovative solutions, knowing that failure is an inherent part of the innovation process.

Prioritize Customer Feedback and Validation:

Prioritize customer feedback and validation to ensure that products, services, or strategies align with customer needs and preferences. Solicit feedback early and often, iterate based on user insights, and validate assumptions through testing and experimentation to mitigate the risk of failure.

Build Resilience and Perseverance:

Build resilience and perseverance to bounce back from failure stronger and more determined than before. Encourage a growth mindset that embraces challenges, setbacks, and failures as opportunities for learning and personal development, fostering resilience and adaptability in the face of adversity.

Learn from Industry Benchmarks and Best Practices:

Learn from industry benchmarks, best practices, and case studies of both successes and failures in your industry. Analyze the strategies, decisions, and outcomes of competitors and industry peers to glean insights, identify trends, and inform your own business practices and decision-making.

Seek Mentorship and Guidance:

Seek mentorship, guidance, and support from experienced entrepreneurs, industry experts, or mentors who can provide valuable perspective, advice, and wisdom based on their own experiences with failure and success.

Celebrate Progress and Successes:

Celebrate progress and successes, no matter how small, to foster a positive and supportive environment within the organization. Recognize and reward employees for their efforts, achievements, and contributions, reinforcing a culture of learning, growth, and resilience.

In conclusion, failures are inevitable in business, but they also present invaluable opportunities for learning, growth, and improvement. By embracing failure as a learning opportunity, identifying failure patterns, fostering a culture of transparency and accountability, and prioritizing innovation and customer feedback, businesses can navigate setbacks, drive continuous improvement, and ultimately achieve success in the face of adversity.

CHAPTER 10.

FUTURE TRENDS IN BUSINESS MODEL DEVELOPMENT

Technological improvements, shifting customer behaviours, and developing market dynamics are all predicted to affect future business model development trends. Key trends include:

Digital Transformation:
Businesses will increasingly use digital technology to simplify processes, improve customer experiences, and drive innovation throughout the business model.

Subscription Economy:
The development of subscription-based models will continue, providing recurring income streams and building long-term client connections through tailored, on-demand services.

Platform Ecosystems:
Platform-based business models will survive by connecting users, suppliers, and partners to generate value and drive network effects.

Sustainability and Purpose:
Businesses will prioritise sustainability, social responsibility, and purpose-driven activities, connecting their business models with environmental and societal aims to fulfill the needs of conscientious customers.

Data Monetization:
As firms use data analytics, artificial intelligence, and machine learning to extract insights, enhance operations, and provide tailored consumer experiences, data-driven business models will become increasingly common.

Collaborative Economy:
The collaborative and sharing economy models will continue to disrupt existing sectors by allowing peer-to-peer transactions and resource sharing via digital platforms.

Flexibe Workforce:
The gig economy will continue to grow as firms implement flexible workforce models and remote work arrangements to react to shifting labour trends and preferences.

Blockchain and Cryptocurrencies:
Blockchain technology and cryptocurrencies will have an impact on business models by allowing safe transactions, decentralized networks, and new monetization options in areas including banking, supply chain, and digital assets.

EMERGING TECHNOLOGIES AND THEIR IMPACT ON BUSINESS

Emerging technologies are altering industries, redefining business structures, and propelling innovation across several sectors. From artificial intelligence to blockchain and beyond, these technologies have the potential to transform the way organizations operate, create value, and engage with their consumers. Here's a thorough look at significant developing technologies and their influence on business:

Artificial Intelligence (AI) and Machine Learning:

AI and machine learning technologies enable organizations to automate jobs, analyze massive volumes of data, and get actionable insights to improve decision-making, optimize processes, and customize consumer experiences. From predictive analytics to chatbots and virtual assistants, AI is changing the way businesses function and interact with their consumer.

Internet of Things (IoT): The internet of things connects actual devices and objects, allowing for real-time monitoring, data collecting, and remote device control. In the commercial world, IoT technologies are driving efficiency improvements, predictive maintenance, and operational optimization in areas including manufacturing, shipping, healthcare, and smart cities.

Blockchain and Distributed Ledger Technology (DLT)

Blockchain and DLT technologies offer safe, transparent, and immutable record-keeping systems that enable peer-to-peer transactions, smart contracts, and decentralized applications. Blockchain has the potential to simplify supply chains, increase traceability, boost cybersecurity, and allow new kinds of digital asset management and tokenization in the corporate world.

Augmented Reality (AR) and Virtual Reality (VR). AR and VR technologies provide immersive digital experiences that combine the actual and virtual worlds, allowing organizations to improve training, visualization, marketing, and consumer interaction. From virtual product presentations to immersive brand experiences, AR and VR are changing the way organizations connect with consumers and stakeholders.

5G Connectivity:

5G technology offers ultra-fast, low-latency connection, allowing for real-time communication, data transmission, and networking across a wide range of devices and applications. In business, 5G networks will allow new use cases such as self-driving cars, remote surgery, augmented reality, and smart infrastructure, transforming sectors and spurring innovation.

Edge Computing:
Edge computing puts computational capacity closer to the data source, allowing for real-time processing, decreased latency, and bandwidth optimization for IoT devices and applications. In business, edge computing enables faster decision-making, improved response times, and enhanced security for mission-critical applications in industries such as manufacturing, healthcare, and transportation.

Biotechnology and genomics:
Biotechnology and genomics technologies are transforming healthcare, agriculture, and environmental sustainability by allowing precision

medicine, gene editing, tailored nutrition, and bio-based manufacturing. In business, biotech discoveries have the potential to disrupt established sectors and open up new avenues for development and innovation.

Quantum Computing:
Quantum computing provides the promise of exponentially quicker processing power and the potential to solve complicated issues that traditional computers cannot currently handle. In business, quantum computing has the potential to transform sectors such as cryptography, optimization, drug development, and materials research, allowing for advances in innovation and discovery.

Impact on Business:
Emerging technologies are fundamentally transforming company models, operations, and consumer experiences. They enable businesses to unlock new revenue streams, improve efficiency, reduce costs, and gain competitive advantage in a

rapidly evolving digital landscape. However, harnessing the full potential of emerging technologies requires strategic vision, investment in talent and infrastructure, and a culture of innovation and experimentation. Businesses that embrace emerging technologies and leverage them effectively will be well-positioned to thrive in the digital age and drive future growth and innovation.

SHIFTING MARKET DYNAMICS: NAVIGATING CHANGE IN THE BUSINESS LANDSCAPE

Market dynamics are the forces and variables that impact the behaviour of consumers and sellers in a market, determining demand, supply, price, competition, and industry structure. Market dynamics in today's fast-paced and linked global economy are continually changing, owing to variables such as technical breakthroughs, legislative changes, economic trends, alterations in consumer behaviour, and competition. Here's a thorough examination of changing market dynamics and their ramifications for businesses:

Technological Advances:
Rapid technology breakthroughs, such as artificial intelligence, the internet of things, and blockchain, are upending sectors, providing new possibilities, and transforming business structures. To be successful in the digital era, businesses must stay up to date on developing technologies, implement digital transformation initiatives, and innovate.

Changing Consumer Behaviors:

Consumer preferences, attitudes, and behaviors are constantly evolving in response to societal trends, cultural shifts, and technological innovations. Businesses must understand their target audience, anticipate changing needs and preferences, and tailor products, services, and experiences to meet evolving customer demands effectively.

Globalization and Market Expansion:

Globalization has expanded market opportunities and intensified competition, as businesses can now reach customers worldwide and access new markets more easily. However, globalization also brings challenges such as increased competition, supply chain complexities, and regulatory hurdles that businesses must navigate to succeed in international markets.

Economic Trends and Cycles:

Economic trends, such as GDP growth, inflation, interest rates, and unemployment, influence consumer spending, business investment, and overall market conditions. Businesses must monitor economic indicators, anticipate economic cycles, and adjust strategies accordingly to mitigate risks and capitalize on opportunities in different economic environments.

Regulatory Changes and Compliance:

Regulatory changes and compliance requirements impact business operations, market entry barriers, and industry dynamics. Businesses must stay informed about regulatory developments, anticipate changes in laws and regulations, and proactively adapt compliance strategies to ensure legal and ethical conduct in their operations.

Competitive Pressures and Industry Disruption:

Competitive pressures and industry disruption are intensifying across various sectors, driven by new entrants, innovative business models, and changing customer expectations. Businesses must continuously assess competitive landscapes, identify potential disruptors, and differentiate themselves through innovation, agility, and customer-centricity to maintain market relevance and competitive advantage.

Environment and Social Responsibility:
Environmental sustainability, social responsibility,

and ethical corporate practices are becoming more essential factors for customers, investors, and stakeholders. Businesses must incorporate sustainability into their company strategy, supply chains, and operations in order to solve environmental issues, fulfill social standards, and foster consumer and stakeholder confidence.

Emerging Risks and Uncertainties: Emerging risks and uncertainties, including geopolitical tensions, cybersecurity attacks, and pandemics, have the potential to disrupt markets, supply chains, and company operations. Businesses must strengthen their resilience, create contingency plans, and use risk management methods to limit possible hazards and maintain business continuity in turbulent circumstances.

Implications for Businesses:

Shifting market dynamics present both difficulties and possibilities for firms, requiring agility, flexibility, and strategic insight to succeed. To compete in an ever-changing market, businesses must embrace innovation, harness digital technology, promote customer-centricity, and cultivate a culture of continuous learning and growth. Businesses that understand and adapt effectively to changing market dynamics may grab opportunities, manage risks, and achieve long-term development and competitiveness in a dynamic and uncertain business environment.

CHAPTER 11.

CONCLUSION AND FINAL THOUGHTS: EMBRACING CHANGE AND DRIVING INNOVATION

Finally, negotiating the intricacies of today's corporate market demands agility, adaptation, and a willingness to welcome change. Throughout this investigation into business model creation, rising technology, evolving market dynamics, and lessons gained from failures, it becomes clear that successful firms are those that consistently innovate, change, and respond successfully to an ever-changing environment.

As organizations face unprecedented challenges and possibilities in the digital era, it is critical to acknowledge that innovation is not only an option, but a must for survival and success. Businesses must be resilient, proactive, and forward-thinking in their approach, whether they are using the potential of emerging technology, pivoting in reaction to market developments, or learning from past missteps.

Finally, the key to success is to establish an organizational culture of invention, cooperation, and continual improvement. Businesses that empower their people to think creatively, experiment with new ideas, and take measured risks may open up new possibilities, create sustainable development, and remain ahead of the curve in an increasingly competitive market.

In the face of uncertainty and change, it is critical to maintain optimism, vision, and adaptability. As we look forward, let us see change as a chance for development, innovation, and transformation. By embracing change, fostering innovation, and being true to our values and purpose, we can create a more resilient future for businesses, communities, and society as a whole.

According to Henry Ford, "Failure is simply the opportunity to begin again, this time more intelligently." Let us accept failure as a stepping stone to success, learn from our mistakes, and move on with tenacity, inventiveness, and perseverance. Together, we can face today's issues and create a successful and sustainable future for future generations.

www.ingramcontent.com/pod-product-compliance
Lightning Source LLC
Chambersburg PA
CBHW050110230526
45470CB00004B/1761